W9-DBH-212

Georgia, My State
Biographies

Coretta Scott King

By Ashleigh Hally

STATE
STANDARDS
PUBLISHING®

Your State • Your Standards • Your Grade Level

Dear Educators, Librarians and Parents . . .

Thank you for choosing this *"Georgia, My State"* series book! We have designed this series to support the Georgia Department of Education's **Common Core Georgia Performance Standards for curriculum studies AND leveled reading**. Each book in the series has been written *at grade level* as measured by the ATOS Readability Formula for Books (Accelerated Reader), the Lexile Framework for Reading, and the Fountas & Pinnell Benchmark Assessment System for Guided Reading. Photographs and/or illustrations, captions, and other design elements have been included to provide supportive visual messaging to enhance text comprehension. Glossary and Word Index sections introduce key new words and help young readers develop skills in locating and combining information. "Think With Bagster" questions provide teachers and parents with tools for additional learning activities and critical thinking development. We wish you all success in using this *"Georgia, My State"* book to meet your student or child's learning needs.

Jill Ward, President

Publisher

State Standards Publishing, LLC
1788 Quail Hollow
Hamilton, GA 31811
USA
1.866.740.3056
www.statestandardspublishing.com

Library of Congress Control Number: 2012931550

ISBN-13: 978-1-935884-78-1 (hardcover)
ISBN-13: 978-1-935884-84-2 (paperback)

Printed in the United States of America, North Mankato, Minnesota, February 2012, 083111.

1 2 3 4 5 - CG - 16 15 14 13 12

About the Author

Ashleigh Hally has a degree in English literature from the University of Georgia. She has been a library assistant and copy-writer and is currently working on a manuscript for the young adult market. She currently teaches reading and writing to elementary students in the Atlanta area. Ashleigh enjoys traveling and spending time with her husband, Patrick, and their three children.

Table of Contents

Hi, I'm Bagster! Let's learn about important Georgia women.

Black people and white people were treated differently in the South.

Unequal Treatment

Coretta Scott was born in Alabama. Black people and white people were treated differently in the South. They could not go to the same schools. They could not use the same water fountains. This was against the law! Coretta's father started his own sawmill for cutting logs. Some people did not want a black man to own a business. They burned down his sawmill!

Coretta picked cotton to make money for her family.

Time Line

1927
Born

1945
Goes to college

Coretta Leaves Home

Coretta picked cotton to make money for her family. But Coretta had a beautiful voice. She went to **college** in Ohio. Students go to college after high school. Coretta studied music. She met students who wanted **civil rights** for black people. They wanted African Americans to be treated the same as white people. Coretta wanted this, too. Coretta and other students worked to change the laws about civil rights.

The Kings started a bus boycott.

Time Line

1927
Born

1945
Goes to college

1955
Starts boycott

Coretta Becomes Mrs. King

Later Coretta went to another school. It was in Boston. She met Martin Luther King, Jr. He was learning to be a **pastor**. He wanted to lead a church. Martin asked Coretta to marry him. She waited six months before she said "yes." Martin got a job at a church. It was in Montgomery, Alabama. The bus company in Montgomery did not treat black people fairly. The Kings started a **boycott**. They asked people not to ride the buses anymore.

Martin and Coretta asked people to protest the Jim Crow laws.

Time Line

1927
Born

1945
Goes to college

1955
Starts boycott

Martin's Partner

Coretta helped Martin with his work. They asked people to **protest**. They gave speeches about peace. They asked people not to follow the **Jim Crow laws**. These laws said it was okay to treat African Americans unfairly. Sometimes people got angry with Coretta and Martin. Once, someone threw a bomb at their house! Coretta was home with her child. They were not hurt.

Ghandi

Coretta and Martin went to India to learn about Ghandi's ideas.

Time Line

1927
Born

1945
Goes to college

1955
Starts boycott

Working for Peace

Martin became famous around the world. Coretta and Martin traveled to different countries. They went to India. They wanted to learn about Mahatma Ghandi. Ghandi taught people to make changes without **violence**. He did not believe in hurting people. Coretta and Martin liked Ghandi's ideas. Later Martin won an award called the **Nobel Peace Prize**. It is given to people who solve problems without violence.

Coretta started Freedom Concerts to raise money for civil rights.

Time Line

1927	1945	1955
Born	Goes to college	Starts boycott

Freedom Concerts

Martin and Coretta moved to Atlanta, Georgia. Martin was a leader in the **civil rights movement**. African Americans wanted to have the same civil rights as white people. Martin was always busy. Coretta wanted to help. She started **Freedom Concerts**. She sang songs at the concerts. She read poems. She told the story of the civil rights movement. Her concerts were a big success.

★ Atlanta

Coretta gave a speech about Martin's work.

Time Line

1927	1945	1955
Born	Goes to college	Starts boycott

Life After Martin

One day, a man killed Martin. Coretta was very sad. She did not want Martin's dream to die, too. Coretta kept speaking out for civil rights. She went to Washington, D. C. She gave a speech about Martin's work. She added her own ideas. Coretta asked people to work together for peace. She said women should be leaders, too. From then on, Coretta had her own dream.

1959
Visits India

1964 Starts
Freedom Concerts

1968
Martin dies

Coretta started The King Center to work for peaceful answers to problems.

Time Line

1927
Born

1945
Goes to college

1955
Starts boycott

Working for Martin's Memory

Coretta started **The King Center**. It is in Atlanta. The people there work for peaceful answers to problems. Coretta also worked to make Martin's birthday a **national holiday**. She wanted everyone to remember Martin's work. She wanted his birthday to be a day to help others. Now we celebrate Martin Luther King, Jr. Day every January.

1959
Visits India

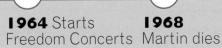

1964 Starts
Freedom Concerts

1968
Martin dies

Some people call Coretta the first lady of the civil rights movement.

Time Line

1927		1945	1955
Born		Goes to college	Starts boycott

A Symbol of Civil Rights

Some people call Coretta Scott King the first lady of the civil rights movement in America. She was a leader. She spoke up for people in other countries, too. She said people should be able to vote for new leaders. People should not be treated differently because of their skin color. Coretta gave people a voice. She worked for the dream of peace.

1959
Visits India

1964 Starts
Freedom Concerts

1968
Martin dies

2006
Coretta dies

21

Glossary

boycott – A type of protest where people agree not to buy a product or use a service.

civil rights – The benefits given to people in a free country.

civil rights movement – A cause that took place during the early 1960s, where people tried to get equal rights for African Americans.

college – A school students attend after high school.

Freedom Concerts – Concerts started by Coretta Scott King to raise money for the civil rights movement.

Jim Crow laws – Laws that allowed unequal treatment of black people.

national holiday – A holiday that is recognized throughout a nation.

Nobel Peace Prize – A famous award given to people who solve problems without violence.

pastor – The leader of a church.

protest – To show that you think a law or rule is wrong.

The King Center – A place Coretta started to work for peaceful answers to problems. The King Center is in Atlanta, Georgia.

violence – Actions that hurt other people by using physical power or force.

Word Index

Editorial Credits

Designer: Michael Sellner, Corporate Graphics, North Mankato, Minnesota

Consultant/Marketing Design: Alison Hagler, Basset and Becker Advertising, Columbus, Georgia

Image Credits — *All images © copyright contributor below unless otherwise specified.*

4/5 – Russell Lee/Wikipedia. **6/7** – Cotton: Library of Congress; Portrait: Photos 12/Alamy. **8/9** – Bettmann/CORBIS. **10/11** – Bettmann/CORBIS. **12/13** – The Kings: Bettmann/CORBIS; Ghandi: Sarah Pett-Noble/Fotolia. **14/15** – Everett Collection Inc./Alamy. **16/17** – Bettmann/CORBIS. **18/19** – King Center: Ian Dagnall/Alamy; MLK,Jr. Day: Margaret Molloy/CORBIS. **20/21** – AllPosters.

Think With Bagster

1. When Coretta was a young girl, black people and white people could not use the same water fountains or bathrooms. How do you think growing up this way prepared Coretta for the work she would do with Martin Luther King, Jr.?

2. Coretta and other civil rights leaders sometimes disobeyed the laws they were trying to change. Is it all right to disobey the law? When? Why do you think this?

3. Do you think a boycott is a good way to protest something that is unfair or wrong? Why or why not?

4. What did Martin and Coretta like about Mahatma Ghandi? How did his message of peace influence the civil rights movement?

5. Why do you think Coretta wanted Martin Luther King, Jr. Day to be a day to help other people?